03-04 10-28-04 Huh

Community Helpers

Radio Announcers

by Panky Snow

Consultant:
William G. Sanders
President
Georgia Association of Broadcasters

Bridgestone Books
an imprint of Capstone Press
Mankato, Minnesota

Bridgestone Books are published by Capstone Press
151 Good Counsel Drive, P.O. Box 669, Mankato, Minnesota 56002
http://www.capstone-press.com

Library of Congress Cataloging-in-Publication Data
Snow, Panky.
    Radio announcers/by Panky Snow.
    p.cm.—(Community helpers)
    Includes bibliographical references and index.
    ISBN 0-7368-0958-9
    1. Radio announcing—Vocational guidance—Juvenile literature. [1. Radio
announcing. 2. Occupations.] I. Title. II. Community helpers (Mankato, Minn.)
PN1991.8.A6 S64 2002
791.44′028′023—dc21   00-012545

Summary: A simple introduction to the work radio announcers do, tools they use, people
    who help them, and their importance to the communities they serve.

Editorial Credits

Sarah Lynn Schuette, editor; Karen Risch, product planning editor; Linda Clavel, cover
    designer; Heidi Schoof, photo researcher

Photo Credits

Capstone Press/Gary Sundermeyer, 8
David F. Clobes, Stock Photography, cover, 4, 6, 14
FPG International LLC, 18
Pictor, 16
Unicorn Stock Photos/Terry Barner, 10; Batt Johnson, 20
Visuals Unlimited/Jeff Greenberg, 12

1 2 3 4 5 6 07 06 05 04 03 02

Table of Contents

Radio Announcers

Radio announcers broadcast news stories and play music on the radio. They talk to radio listeners. Some radio announcers read from a script. Scripts tell radio announcers what to say.

broadcast
to give or to report information on the radio

What Radio Announcers Do

Radio announcers research and report news. They choose music to play. Some radio announcers give weather forecasts. They sometimes interview people on radio shows.

forecast
what someone thinks will happen in the future

Where Radio Announcers Work

Radio announcers work at radio stations. They sit or stand in studios. Studios are soundproof. Some radio shows broadcast live from stores or outdoor events. Radio announcers sometimes report news stories as they happen.

soundproof
without outside noise

Types of Radio Announcers

Disc jockeys play audiotapes and CDs on the radio. Weather reporters give forecasts. Sportscasters give scores and comment on games. Some radio announcers host talk shows.

Tools Radio Announcers Use

Radio announcers speak into a microphone. Some radio announcers record events on audiotape. They also use CDs to play music and computers to play commercials.

microphone

an instrument used to record sound or to make sound louder

Skills Radio Announcers Need

Radio announcers need good speaking skills. They need to read scripts clearly and correctly. Radio announcers should have good research skills. Many radio announcers research news stories on the Internet.

Internet
a connection of computer networks all over the world

How Radio Announcers Learn

Some people learn how to be radio announcers by working at radio stations. Other people who want to be radio announcers go to college. They take classes to learn how to speak well.

college
a place where students study after high school

17

People Who Help Radio Announcers

Program directors work with radio announcers to decide what music to play. Sound technicians make sure microphones are working correctly. Listeners ask radio announcers to play certain music. Listeners also ask questions.

How Radio Announcers Help Others

Radio announcers tell listeners about the news and the weather. They entertain listeners with music. Radio announcers often report emergencies such as storms and floods. Radio announcers help listeners stay safe.

entertain
to provide something interesting or enjoyable

Hands On: Make Radio Sound Effects

In the past, radio announcers made their own sound effects from everyday objects. Today, radio announcers use computers to make sound effects. This activity will show you how to make your own sound effects.

What You Need

Empty round oatmeal box
1 cup uncooked rice or dried peas
Thin metal cookie sheet
Paper towel tube
Large box filled with small rocks and sand

What You Do

1. Pour the cup of rice or peas into the oatmeal box. Put the lid on the box and shake the box lightly to make the sound of soft rain. Shake the box faster for a rain storm.
2. Hold one end of the cookie sheet and shake it to make the sound of thunder.
3. Blow into one end of the paper towel tube to make the sound of wind.
4. Stand in the box filled with sand and rocks. Move your feet to make the sound of someone walking.

What other sound effects can you make?

Words to Know

audiotape (AW-dee-oh-tape)—a magnetic tape that records sound

commercial (kuh-MUR-shuhl)—a short radio message that tells about a business or a product

emergency (e-MUR-juhn-see)—a sudden or dangerous event

script (SKRIPT)—a written plan for a radio show; scripts tell radio announcers what to say.

studio (STOO-dee-oh)—a place where radio shows and recordings are made; radio announcers work in soundproof studios.

technician (tek-NISH-uhn)—someone who works with and fixes equipment; sound technicians make sure microphones work correctly.

Read More

Chambers, Catherine. *Radio.* Behind Media. Chicago: Heinemann Library, 2001.

Dubois, Muriel L. *I Like Music: What Can I Be?* Mankato, Minn.: Bridgestone Books, 2001.

Internet Sites

Brain Pop: Radio Movie
http://www.brainpop.com/tech/communication/radio/index.weml
Disc Jockey
http://stats.bls.gov/k12/html/mus_006.htm
What Does a Radio Announcer Do?
http://www.whatdotheydo.com/radio_an.htm

Index